MW01295725

This Journal Belongs To

_____

ISBN-13: 9781098737009

**Artwork By Tamer Elsharouni
and Cindy Elsharouni**
Copyright 2019 © Selah Works
The copyrights of these images are
owned by Selah Works. All Rights Reserved.
Cover By Tamer Elsharouni
No part of this book or these pages may
be reproduced, distributed or transmitted
in any way without prior written permission
of Selah Works. www.selahworks.com

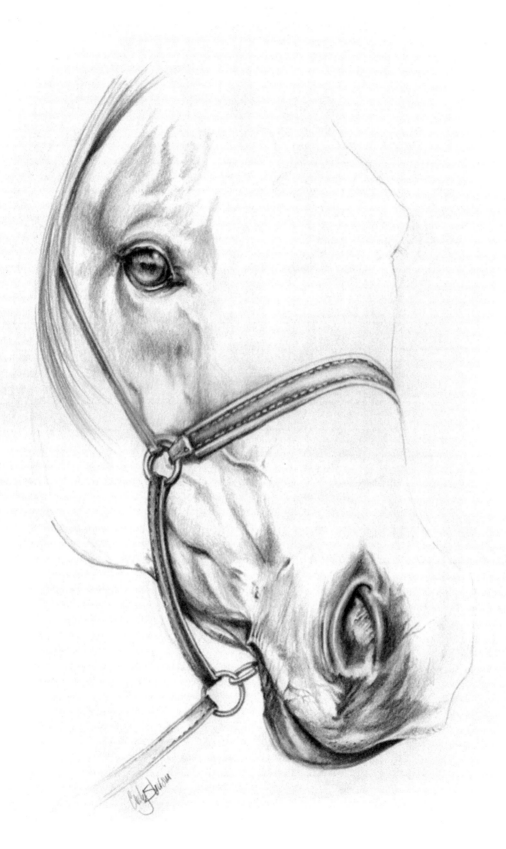

The essential joy of being with horses is that it brings us in contact with the rare elements of grace, beauty, spirit and freedom.

Sharon Ralls Lemon

The path

to my heart

is paved with

hoofprints.

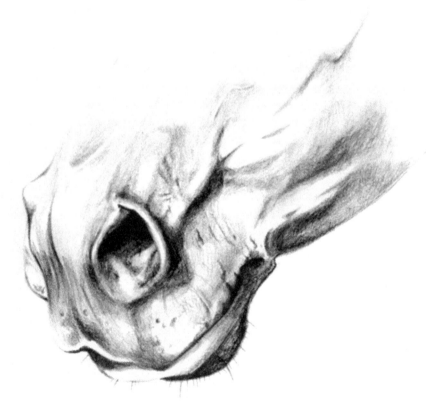

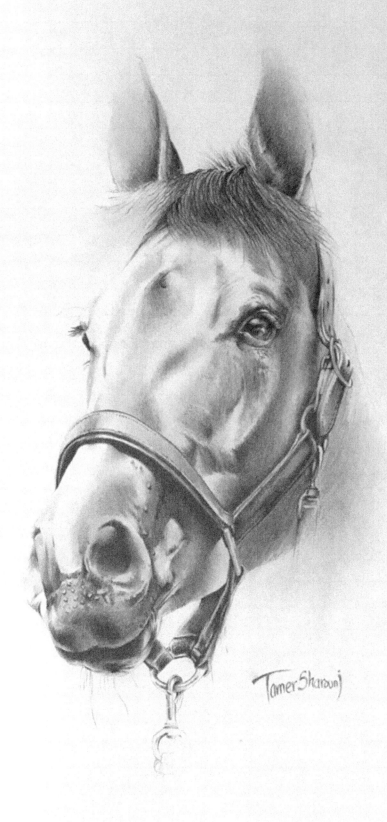

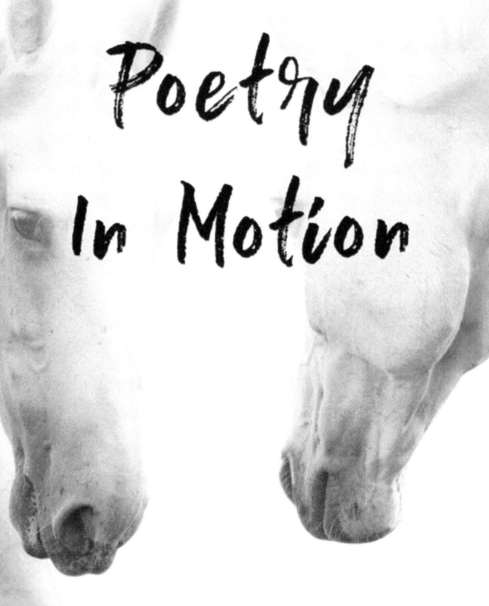

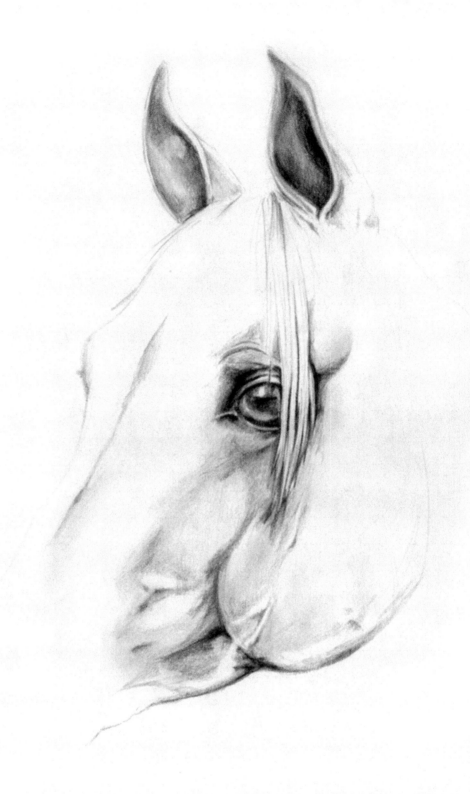

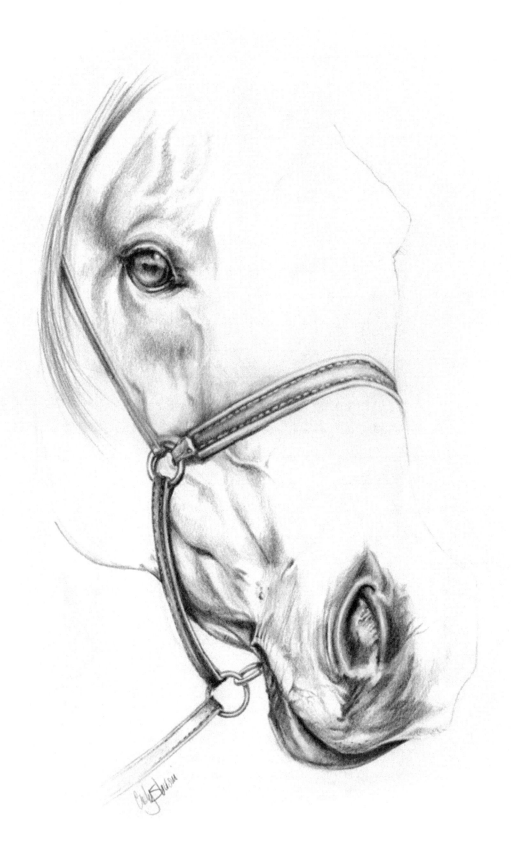

Made in the USA
Columbia, SC
17 November 2020